Postwar Aircraft

Osprey Modelling Manuals
Volume 12

Rodrigo Hernández Cabos

OSPREY

Osprey Modelling Manuals 12

POSTWAR AIRCRAFT

First published in Great Britain in 2000 by Osprey Publishing,
Elms Court, Chapel Way, Botley, Oxford OX2 9LP, United Kingdom.
Email: info@ospreypublishing.com

© Acción Press, S. A., C/Ezequiel Solana, 16, 28017, Madrid, Spain.
   Euromodelismo. Depósito Legal M-19729-1992.

ISBN 1 84176 159 1

English edition packaged by Compendium, 1st Floor, 43 Frith Street,
London, W1V 5TE

00 01 02 03 04 10 9 8 7 6 5 4 3 2 1

Publication Manager: Rodrigo Hernández Cabos
Photographs: Salvador Gómez Mico, Rodrigo Hernández Cabos
Modelling Team: Cristóbal Vergara Durán, Julio C. Cabos Gómez,
Juan M. Villalba Domínguez, Rafael Jimenez Rodríguez

Printed in Spain

*For a catalogue of all books published by Osprey Military and
Aviation please contact:*

**The Marketing Manager, Osprey Direct UK, PO Box 140,
Wellingborough, Northants, NN8 4ZA, United Kingdom.
Tel. (0)1933 443863, Fax (0)1933 443849.
Email: info@ospreydirect.co.uk**

**The Marketing Manager, Osprey Direct USA, PO Box 130,
Sterling Heights, MI 48311-0130, USA. Tel. 248 394 6191,
Fax 248 394 6194. Email: info@ospreydirectusa.com**

Visit Osprey at:
www.ospreypublishing.com

INTRODUCTION

e beauty of modelling post-World War II aircraft can be summed up simply: jets, helicopters
nd missiles. Unlike World War II, where almost everything was prop-driven, the postwar
ars are the years of the jet. In the postwar years the jet has developed into a superlative
wer source, enabling postwar designers to go to places barely imaginable in 1945. Attack
helicopters, V/STOL (vertical/short take-off), variable geometry wings — and what
weaponry. Modern aircraft are always groaning under a fascinating array of pods and
dispensers — heat-seeking Sidewinders, anti-radar HARMs, ECM and ESM pods, anti-tank
missiles, gun pods and drop tanks.

is twelfth book in the Osprey Modelling Manual series looks at an range of modern aircraft
— the US Navy's hottest fighter-bombers, the F-14 Tomcat and F-18 Hornet; V/STOL in the
rm of a Spanish AV-8B Harrier; European versatility with the RAF's F3 Tornado, and classics
om the Eastern Bloc: the beautiful MiG-29 'Fulcrum' and Su-27 'Flanker-B' interceptors; the
variable-geometry Su-24 'Fencer', the best ground-attack aircraft in the world, the Su-25
rogfoot', and ; finally, there's a heavyweight attack helicopter, the Kamov Ka-50 'Hokum'.

The art of modern aircraft modelling is attention to detail — superdetailing of cockpits,
undercarriage, weaponry and panelling; weathering meticulously applied paintwork; and
ensuring complete realism with the variety of transfers (decals) needed. Now read on . . .

SUKHOI Su-25

The project for the Su-25 was born in the late 1960s, with a competition being held to equip the Soviet air force with a reaction plane specifically devoted to ground support missions — furthermore it had to have a simple design and come in at a low cost.

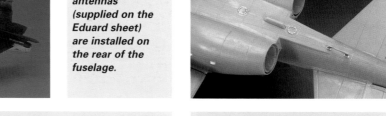

The three etched-brass antennas (supplied on the Eduard sheet) are installed on the rear of the fuselage.

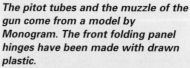

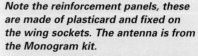

Place the rear-view mirrors on the front strut of the cockpit canopy. Note that the central windscreen is blue, painted with transparent blue from Tamiya.

The pitot tubes and the muzzle of the gun come from a model by Monogram. The front folding panel hinges have been made with drawn plastic.

Note the reinforcement panels, these are made of plasticard and fixed on the wing sockets. The antenna is from the Monogram kit.

Sukhoi built a prototype aircraft, the T-8-1, which was much better than the previous Ilyushin project, the Il-102. Various other prototypes were built, until they reached the fourth, the T-8-4, which differed considerably from the first in terms of its engines, modified nozzles, the position of the gun, the dihedral stabilisers, etc. This aeroplane was very similar to the current model.

The first production versions of the T-8 were sent to Afghanistan to be evaluated. They proved to be highly useful, because they could carry out their mission orders much better than the MiG-21, mainly because of their better bomb load. They were generally armed with bombs ranging from 100 to 250kg, rocket launchers up to 320mm calibre and sub-munitions containers.

The current Su-25s differ slightly from the T-8 — but the differences are because of experience won in battle. Due to the use of modern anti-aircraft missiles by the Afghan Mujaheddin, some units were shot down and lost over Afghanistan. Following these losses Sukhoi introduced a number of improvements to the original design, including the installation of a fire bulkhead between the engines to prevent the loss or explosion of one from damaging the other. The number of flare launchers was also increased considerably; these were housed in pods installed on the engine nacelles. Since making these changes, no other T-8 was completely lost.

Thanks to these improvements, the Su-25's survival in combat increased considerably. Some aircraft were able to return to base with one engine totally destroyed; one aircraft came back with a Sidewinder AAM (shot by a Pakistani F-16) embedded in it.

As well as the former USSR,

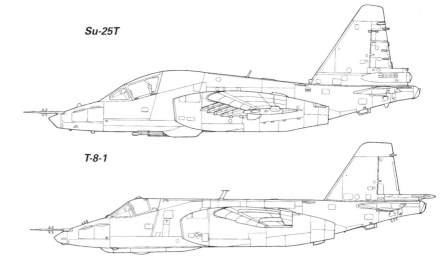

Su-25T

T-8-1

The AA-8 missile comes from the Monogram kit. Some of its details have been made using plasticard.

The folding access panel in the lower section of the central gun container is built with plasticard.

The main undercarriage is from Monogram. The fuel tank tabs have been reconstructed with plasticard.

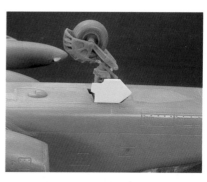

The front undercarriage combines parts from Oez and Monogram. The gate is made of plasticard.

Initially it was offered to the Russian air forces to replace the L-39 Albatross, but although it proved to be better, it was rejected for economic reasons.

The Su-25BM is basically an Su-25 adapted to tow a target pod (white) under its wings for shooting practice. The Su-25UGT is the navalised version of the Su-25UT, fitted with a rear hook for landing on aircraft carriers.

Although the design of the Su-25 is reliable, it is also rather basic, so Russian pilots soon requested a more complex version to include all types of modern weapons. For this, Sukhoi devised the Su-25T, which used a two-seat version but without rear seat so that new fuel tanks could be added instead, as well as more capable ECM equipment. The number of chaff-launchers was increased and infra-red camouflage equipment, night vision pods, etc. were installed. The Su-25T was also fitted with the long-range, laser-guided new 'Vikhr' anti-tank missile. This model was offered for export because Russian forces were unable to accept it for obvious economic reasons.

other countries use the Su-25. It was exported to former Czechoslovakia and Bulgaria (as the Su-25K). Iraq also received some but with degraded systems and equipment. A significant number of variants exist. The Su-25UB is a two-seat training version, with the same offensive capacity as the single-seater, but with less autonomy.

The Su-25UT (or Su-28) is an unarmed version of the Su-25UB, devised for basic pilot training.

However, until proved otherwise, the Su-25 is rated among the best anti-tank aircraft in the world.

THE SCALE MODEL

At the moment there are two kits of the Sukhoi Su-25 in ⅟₄₈ scale: one is from Oez and the other from Monogram. After comparing the two models, we have chosen to make the one from the Czech company, because it scrupulously respects all the dimensions — and is particularly good in terms of its panels and body shape.

This is not to say that the Monogram kit is faulty; indeed, it has a couple of extra centimetres on the fuselage and on each wing. Also the small pieces, such as the wheels, pressure heads,

The gun muzzle fairing is painted matt aluminium over the pale blue applied on the lower surfaces.

The laser rangefinder is housed on the nose. The tabs of the pressure head are etched brass.

The K-36 seat is from Verlinden. The cockpit canopy restraint link was made using drawn plastic.

The beige-coloured lines on the struts of the windscreen and the cockpit canopy were made with transfer strips.

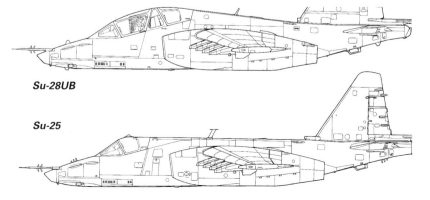

Su-28UB

Su-25

undercarriage, etc, are better reproduced than those from Oez.

The quality of both models can be improved — especially inside the cockpit — with the resin kit from Verlinden that reproduces the K-36 seat; this is the best, simply because Verlinden is the only manufacturer to supply it! The second kit is the Eduard etched-brass one. This includes a large number of pieces and is unbeatable value for money. Unfortunately Eduard kits can be hard to track down.

It is much easier to assemble and paint the interior of the cockpit in stages. Assembling everything at once would be much quicker, but would cause complications later.

Once the cockpit was finished, we moved on to assemble the wings. These need attaching with panels projecting from the lining; we made these with very thin plasticard.

The undercarriage needs an some improvement, especially the rear unit. To resolve this problem we had to use the most expensive but most effective formula — cannibalising pieces from a Monogram model. To all the weapon supports under the wings we added some semi-circular bulking, 12mm in length, made with rods from Contrail or Evergreen. On the nose a small circular hole must be made to house the laser rangefinder. Once the whole kit is assembled, added the last pieces of etched brass.

The air brakes incorporate a landing light and small anti-static cables on the ends. These were made with drawn plastic.

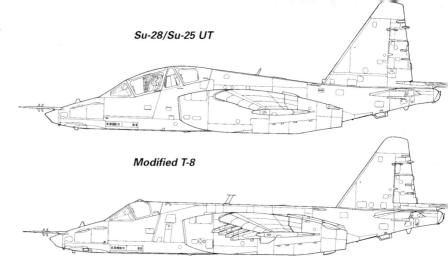

Su-28/Su-25 UT

Modified T-8

The green used on the hub of the main undercarriage is 'dark green wheel hub' from Xtracolor (X-628).

A well sharpened pencil was used to mark the panel lines.

The sockets of the flaps were masked and then highlighted using an airbrush and sepia inks.

The white strip on the rear of the fuselage was made with the help of masking tape.

PAINTING

The camouflage scheme reproduced here was published in issue 2 of the Czechoslovakian magazine *Zlinek* in 1990. It belonged to a Soviet unit during the 'Kavkaz 88' manoeuvres involving Warsaw Pact countries.

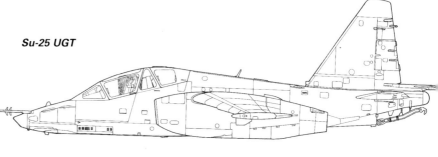

Su-25 UGT

Su-25s belonging to the Slovakian Air Force. After the split into two different states, both republics have shared the former Czech air force equipment proportionally. (Photo: Cristóbal Vergara Durán)

Front instrument panel. Although most are analogue, they are reliable and precise. (Photo: Cristóbal Vergara Durán)

Right side of the cockpit. The red handles are part of the ejection seat. (Photo: Cristóbal Vergara Durán)

Detail of the HUD — head-up display. The aluminium-coloured accessory is a camera. (Photo: Michael Abanshin)

The modernised T-8 and Su-25 have a pair of flare launchers on each engine nacelle. (Photo: Karl-Heinz Feller)

Detail of the APU-62-1M launcher, for the R-60 infra-red missile (AA-80). (Photo: Karl-Heinz Feller)

Nose of an Su-25. Note the two gates that house avionics equipment. (Photo: Karl-Heinz Feller)

The white band on the fuselage indicates that the aeroplane was acting as an 'enemy'. We used enamel type paints, mainly from Humbrol. Aviation Blue (no 65) was used to paint the lower surfaces. The upper scheme, using four tones, is composed of Earth colour (no 63), Marine Green (no 105), Brass Green (no 75) and Dark Earth (LF-3 from Mo-Lak). Inside the cockpit, the nozzles and undercarriage shafts were painted Pale Grey (no 147), and on the weapon, Matt Aluminium (no 56).

To paint the antennas and radomes, we used Japanese

Front undercarriage showing the typical Sukhoi mudguards. (Photo: Cristóbal Vergara Durán)

The air brake system deployed. The landing light can also be seen. (Photo: Jaromir Stepan)

Sukhoi Su-25K of the Czechoslovakian Air Force. The very showy paintwork was done specially for the Boscombe Air Festival in 1992. (Photo: Daniel Vasut)

Unarmed Sukhoi Su-28 (Su-25UT) at the Farnborough Airshow. (Photo: Cristóbal Vergara Durán)

Green (XF-13 from Tamiya), and for the wheel hubs and front wheel protector Xtra Color X-628. The painting is done in the usual way, beginning with the pale colours and finishing with the darker ones. Templates were used for the outlines of the camouflage. Once the model was painted, it was varnished

Left side showing undercarriage detail. (Photo: Jaromir Stepan)

General view of the nose of a Czech Su-25. The steps are built into the structure of the aircraft. (Photo: Jaromir Stepan)

An Su-25 'Frogfoot' in flight. Note the aggressive shark's mouth painted on the nose. (Photo: Daniel Vasut)

The design of the tail plane is unique in a fighter plane as it incorporates two rudders. (Photo: Cristóbal Vergara Durán)

with a gloss finish and the panels were detailed using a very sharp pencil.

Using masks, sepia inks and an airbrush we highlighted all the mobile surfaces such as the rudder, tails and flaps. Wear and tear effects were also added on the lower surfaces and the nozzles using an airbrush and fine brushes. When all this was dry we applied the transfers and the entire aeroplane was matt varnished. The beige lines on the struts of the cockpit canopy were made from painted pieces of colourless transfer, carefully placed one by one.

A Sukhoi Su-25K in Rondice. The open access point to the 30mm canon can be clearly seen. (Photo: Daniel Vasut).

F-14 TOMCAT

The Grumman F-14 Tomcat is one of the best known
aircraft currently used by the United States Navy. A major contribution to thi
fame has come from top box office success in movies such as *Top Gun*, in
which the true stars are the aeroplanes. Here we have modelled
an F-14A from aircraft carrier USS *Enterprise*.

THE SCALE MODEL

This is an excellent model, in ½
scale, from the Japanese
company Hasegawa. All the
pieces are correct, with a
remarkably high degree of
detail, considering the scale.
Nevertheless, we can still
improve the aeroplane.

ASSEMBLY AND DETAILING

First, as usual when making any
scale model, we searched for
source information on and
photographs of the model to be
built. It is not difficult to find
abundant documentation on the
F-14 in any specialist bookshop.
In this case, we used the
Encyclopedia of Aviation, fro
Delta, volume I; *F-14 Tomcat
Action*, by Lou Drendel, fro
Squadron Signal Publication
plus a large quantity of photo
obtained from various sources.

We assembled the mod
following the instructions fro
the kit.

COCKPIT AND PILOT

The cockpit is very detailed, an
even has several engrave
pieces, such as the instrume
panels, which are also supplie
as transfers (decals).

We began by assembling th
pilot and radio operator's panel
which we then detailed wit
copper wire, brass an
plasticard. Some grips an
straps are oversized, so w
eliminated them and instea
swapped them for others that w
made ourselves.

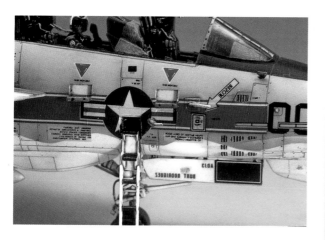

Low adhesion tape was used to mask the different areas of colour.

Side detail of the cockpit with ladder and footrests in the open position. Note the huge number of transfers (decals).

The central part of the windscreen is painted with transparent blue paint. The lines of panels and rivets were marked with an HB propelling pencil.

The radio operator is from Verlinden. His safety belts are made with small brass strips and the buckles with thin copper wire.

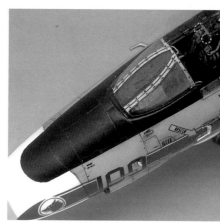

SHAFTS, UNDERCARRIAGE AND NOZZLES

The radio operator's seat has to be adapted to accommodate a figure. We chose a resin one from Verlinden from a kit of pilots and maintenance crew belonging to the United States Navy. In spite of its high price, the quality of the figures makes its worthwhile.

With a sharp knife we removed the safety belts from the seat, then sanded it down to make it uniform. Then, with a punch, we re-marked the details on again. The figure was glued in place with cyanoacrylate; the details include some safety belts made of fine brass strips with buckles made of very fine copper wire.

The tube of the radio operator's mask is made from very fine copper wire wound onto another thicker wire and glued with cyanoacrilate.

The remainder of the cockpit hardly needs detailing; just add some small home-made handles and levers.

We painted the cockpit with Humbrol enamels following the instructions given in the kit.

The front instrument panels deserve special attention. Once painted, each instrument was gloss-varnished; then all the instruments were cut from each transfer, one by one, and glued in place using Micro Sol and Micro Set. We then painted over all with matt varnish and finally added a drop of Alquil to each of the clocks and instruments, to achieve very realistic results.

The shafts and undercarriage were improved by adding cables and small clamps, which we made with drawn plastic rods. These were then painted before being glued into place.

We began with an airbrushed base coat of Tamiya chocolate brown. Then, with enamels and with a pale grey (Humbrol no 64), we brush-painted the raised areas, blurring the colour with a fine brush which was slightly damped with thinner. Note that the brown must show through

General detail of the cockpit. The majority of the oversized handles and straps have been replaced with other, much smaller, ones. The inside of the cockpit is painted with Humbrol enamels.

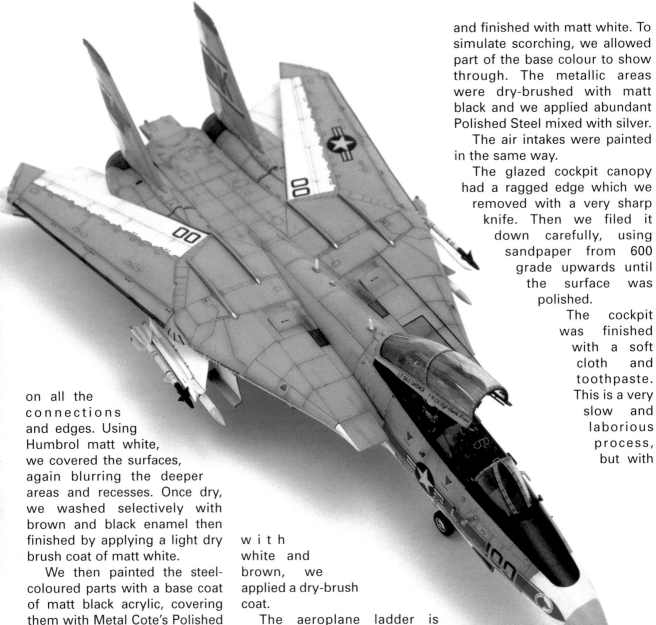

and finished with matt white. To simulate scorching, we allowed part of the base colour to show through. The metallic areas were dry-brushed with matt black and we applied abundant Polished Steel mixed with silver.

The air intakes were painted in the same way.

The glazed cockpit canopy had a ragged edge which we removed with a very sharp knife. Then we filed it down carefully, using sandpaper from 600 grade upwards until the surface was polished.

The cockpit was finished with a soft cloth and toothpaste. This is a very slow and laborious process, but with

on all the connections and edges. Using Humbrol matt white, we covered the surfaces, again blurring the deeper areas and recesses. Once dry, we washed selectively with brown and black enamel then finished by applying a light dry brush coat of matt white.

We then painted the steel-coloured parts with a base coat of matt black acrylic, covering them with Metal Cote's Polished Steel, and finally polishing them with a soft chamois leather.

The wheels of the under-carriage were painted separately. We covered the rubber tires with matt black enamel, filling the gaps with dark grey (Humbrol no 125); then, mixing this grey

with white and brown, we applied a dry-brush coat.

The aeroplane ladder is slimmed down with watch-maker's files and sandpaper, making a series of drill holes in the sides with a 0.5mm bit.

The insides of the nozzles were airbrushed with Tamiya brown acrylic. This was followed by several coats of pale cream

patience it can achieve stupendous results and so is well worth the time and effort you put in.

The shafts and undercarriage units are improved by adding cables and small clamps made from drawn plastic rods. It is best to paint them before gluing them into position.

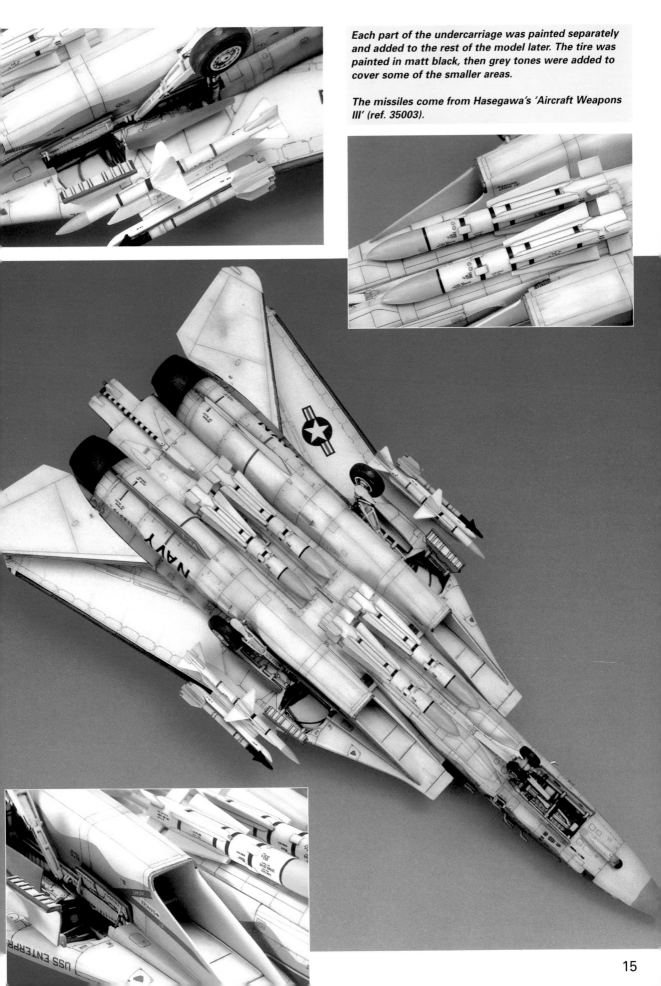

Each part of the undercarriage was painted separately and added to the rest of the model later. The tire was painted in matt black, then grey tones were added to cover some of the smaller areas.

The missiles come from Hasegawa's 'Aircraft Weapons III' (ref. 35003).

WEAPONS

These are not included in the kit; however, in the instructions there are various options to follow. We wanted to include a missile, which we took from the Hasegawa 'Aircraft Weapons III' — a kit collection of good quality weapons. These only needed a slight lowering of the tails — easily done with a watchmaker's file and sandpaper. (The mechanic is also by Hasegawa.)

The assembly of the rest of the plane is straightforward; we only needed to cover the joins with a layer of putty and then sand them down.

PAINTING AND FINISHING

We started by masking the model with Scotch adhesive tape, after reducing its stickiness somewhat.

Using cotton and Maskol we masked the cockpit, the under carriage shafts, the air intakes and nozzles.

The first priming was by airbrush and a mixture of Tamiya acrylics (75% J.N. Grey XF-12 + 25% Flat Black XF-1).

As the camouflage of the aeroplane uses two tones, we started with the paler one. With white acrylic (Tamiya Flat White XF-2) we covered the area panel by panel, taking care that they were highlighted with the base colour. Next, using an airbrush filled with a mixture of brown and cream, we edged the lines of the panels and rivets

The lines of panels and rivets on the grey are emphasised with a medium hard HB pencil.

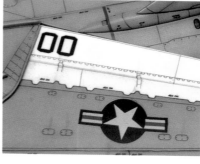

Detail of the wing. Note the grey and black masking which follows the detail of the piece.

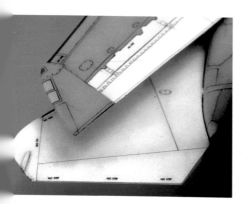

On the white surfaces we edged the lines of the panels with an airbrush, using a mixture of brown and cream.

The aeroplane ladder is slimmed down using watchmaker's files and sandpaper. A series of holes was made in the sides with a 0.5mm drill bit.

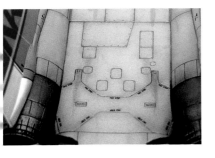

Rear area of the fuselage at its point of connection with the nozzles. The effects of wear (applied with an airbrush) must not be overdone.

Detail of the grey tailplane with its white rudder. Note the position of the different transfers.

Lower view with the landing hook and the engine nozzles, painted with a brown acrylic base.

then with the mouthpiece of the airbrush open, we moved it about 30–40cm away and sprayed acrylic white paint. This serves to soften the contrasts and make the highlighting of the panels very subtle.

We masked the underside of the aeroplane with Scotch tape, cutting the correct lengths with a sharp knife. It was painted following the same system, but instead of white we used J.N. Grey (XF-12).

Masks were made so that the nose and the front edge of the cockpit could be painted with an airbrush.

Next, with an HB pencil for the grey and a 2H for the white, we marked the lines of panels and rivets. After this, with very diluted Humbrol enamel paint and a fine brush, we 'dirtied' the plane. To do this we used small quantities of brown and black, wetting the brush then dabbing it dry it with a paper towel until it left very delicate and blurred marks.

Detail of the missiles with their corresponding supports. They have been painted separately and added to the kit later — this makes the painting of the wings easier.

We painted all the remaining details with a brush: the nozzles matt black and Polished Steel, applying a light coat of silver with a dry brush. Simulated scorch marks were airbrushed with light touches of sepia and grey inks.

Then the entire aircraft was glossed with Marabú varnish. Over this base we placed the transfers using Micro Set and Micro Sol glues. To hide their edges, we cut them level with a knife and ruler and replaced the smaller ones with Verlinden transfers.

Next we mounted the weapons, the undercarriage, etc, (already separately painted), and glued them to the plane. This is the stage at which to do all the touching-up and to 'dirty' some of the transfers.

The penultimate job is to varnish the entire plane with a 50% mixture of Marabú gloss and matt varnish. Then the only thing to do is to remove the masking from the transparent parts and glue the glazed cockpit canopy to the cockpit.

KAMOV Ka-50 HOKUM

The Ka-50 is produced in ½ scale by Italeri and Dragon, although recently Revell has also launched a kit of this helicopter as a new line.

The Kamov Ka-50 is the new Russian attack helicopter incorporating original features that are unparalleled in Western air forces.

The scale model from Dragon is a typical product by this manufacturer, with the panel lines finely engraved into the model, a good general level of detail and a complete sheet of transfers; however, the model has some defective shapes and assembly problems.

The kit by Italeri is less expensive and offers excellent quality as regards its details; inconveniently, however, the panel lines are engraved to face outwards. To improve this model, it would be necessary to eliminate all the original relief work and re-engrave it onto the plastic again — too laborious and complex an operation even for the most die-hard enthusiast, particularly as the scale model by

The glass of the front windscreen is completely painted with transparent blue acrylic.

It is just possible to see the armour plating inside the cockpit through the glass.

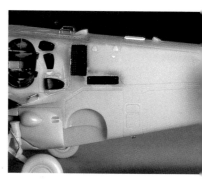

The ventilation grids have been hollowed out with a milling cutter and replaced with plastic mesh.

The handles have been rebuilt from copper wire.

To insert the rotor by Italeri in the Dragon model, you need to modify the piece into which the vertical shaft is inserted.

The hydraulic pipes of the undercarriage and the gun have been made with very fine copper wire.

Dragon is available. The best solution (although most expensive) is to build a hybrid Ka-50 from both models.

The fuselage used is the one from Dragon, as are the interior pieces of the cockpit, which we painted with pale naval grey (Humbrol M-141). The interior of the transparent piece for the front windscreen is painted with a mixture of 70% gloss varnish and 30% translucent blue (Tamiya X-23), simulating the blue cast of the reinforced glass. The seat is completely black, with the safety harness coloured

The double rotor set and the vanes come from the Italeri model, and are much better detailed than those from the Dragon kit.

In the nose area, it is necessary to remove the original sensor and adapt the shape of the Italeri kit.

THE KAMOV KA-50 SCALE MODEL

(Kits in injected plastic, currently in production)

Brand	Scale	Ref no
DRAGON	½	2509
ESCI	½	9073
ITALERI	½	031
REVELL	½	4406

desert yellow (M-93). The work on the interior is completed by adding the support of the head-up display, some cables and the small lateral plates of armour that show through the glass.

Before assembling the two halves of the fuselage, we hollowed out with a milling cutter all the ventilation grilles located in the nacelles of the engines, replacing them with a fine non-metallic mesh.

The piece onto which we fit the rotor shaft must be modified to couple it with the Italeri scale model, which is much more correct and better detailed. The Dragon kit includes a sensor under the nose, for which there is no photographic evidence, so we ignored it and instead adapted the Italeri model.

The gun needs the most detailing as it has no fairing and all the hydraulic pipes, cables and mechanisms, which are omitted in the model, are visible. With copper wire, plasticard and flexible tube from Verlinden we compensated for this loss. The colours to use are pale blue, aluminium, pale green and, of course, metallic grey for the gun. We used the weapon and supports from Italeri; this kit also provided the front undercarriage.

PAINTING

We had two options on how to paint the Ka-50: the first is in the camouflage colour used by the initial prototypes. The second option is based on a rather funereal scheme with black on all the surfaces. We opted for the former, although in this case we will need to add on the left side of the nose a small additional test probe, which can be built with fine plastic rods by Contrail or Evergreen; this probe was mounted on all those pre-production aircraft that carried a camouflage paint scheme.

The colour to use for the underside surfaces is aviation blue (Humbrol M-65), while the camouflage is composed of the colours Stone (Xtracolor X-604 Mi-24) and Dark Grey-Green (X-605 Mi-24) with a brown (M-118) mark on the tail and black (M-33) on the nose. The double rotor is decorated with a priming of Pale Naval Grey (M-141), on which we repainted the blades and part of the rotor with Medium Grey (M-145) and the arms of the blades with Orange (M-82). The anti-tank missiles are painted

The pods mounted on the internal posts come from the 'Soviet Armaments no 2' kit by Dragon.

The anti-tank missiles have been painted reddish-brown (Humbrol M-160).

with Reddish-Brown (M-16) and the wheel hubs, with Wheel Hub Green (X-68).

In the internal posts, two VPK-23-250 pods, included in the 'Soviet Armament kit no. 2' from Dragon, have been mounted. Templates cut out of Bristol board have been used to define the different shapes of the camouflage areas. After applying a layer of gloss varnish, we placed on the Dragon transfers and marked the panel lines with a pencil, finally matt varnishing the entire model at the end.

The colour used to paint the underside is Aviation Blue (Humbrol M-65).

The socket section of the rotor blade arms is painted a strident orange.

To apply the camouflage, always start with the paler colour as the base, adding the green, black and brown areas on top of this.

Once the colours of the camouflage have been applied, decorate the small details of the model with a brush.

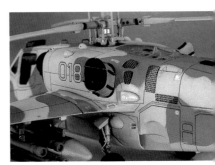

The colours of the camouflage have been applied with an airbrush, delineating the outline of the patches with paper or Bristol board stencils.

Before applying the final matt varnish, highlight the lines of the panels with a pencil.

F-18C HORNET

After a visit to the air base of Torrejón — where we compiled an impressive quantity of data on the F-18 which complemented the excellent books available on the market — we could not resist the temptation to make a super-detailed model.

We took as our base Hasegawa's kit of the F-18C. To enhance it we used a Verlinden etched-brass and resin accessory kit. The scale model is quite good, but it has fitting problems, which we will discuss later. The Verlinden kit is the ideal complement as it offers enough material to improve the cockpit and internal details, fuselage, radar, weapon hardpoints and the weapons themselves.

We started by separating the pieces from their plastic spars, removing any rough edges and imperfections. Then we started the transformation. We used a knife to cut away the leading edge flaps; for the trailing edge we used a saw, since in this area the plastic is much thicker.

We also used the saw to cut into the lower fuselage to improve the compartment for radar and avionics and the ammunition feed, as well as the folding wings and the fuelling point. Similarly, we separated the cone that covers the radar from the part corresponding to the muzzle of the gun, using a 0.1mm saw blade. Finally, we hollowed out the side avionics compartment with a knife, finishing this off using a file.

After finishing this phase, we began work on the cockpit starting with kit piece B-4 — the floor and side consoles. Unfortunately, the latter are so narrow that they will not take the instrumentation transfers and so need a lot of modification.

To solve this problem, we added rectangles of 1mm thick plasticard and a rectangular cover of 0.1mm thick plasticard. These two pieces provided the base for completely new consoles. Unfortunately the Verlinden etched-brass detailing kit did not help us a great deal here; its detailing, too, is poor, so we made the consoles and a front panel using 0.1mm plasticard. The end result — overlapping sheets of plasticard — is very good; we finished by painting them matt black, and highlighting with a dry brush and a medium grey.

Luckily the resin seat is very good, but because the harness and belts are moulded in the same material we used the kit original, which we improved by

Detail of the gun air intake and ventilation hatches.

A very important piece that needs careful detailing is the folding-wing hinge.

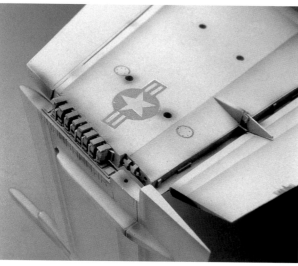

The wing hinge is constructed with thin sheets of plastic made by Evergreen.

Practically all the moving parts are cut and rotated from their original position: note the trailing edge flaps.

using the Verlinden example as the model. We added the pieces separately, so that it looked more authentic. Belts and buckles were made using 0.1mm brass and copper sheets; copper electrical wire was used for the ejection seat rails with sections by Evergreen; canvas for the seat was backed with tin sheet, a little thicker than

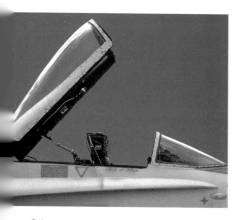

The glazed cockpit canopy is heavily detailed with additional wiring and rear-view mirrors.

previously, to which we added relief using a knife and/or punch.

We continued detailing the cockpit with the addition of the levers, HUD and wiring.

The rear cockpit needs a lot of work: piece D-12 covers this area in a haphazard way, and the etched-brass component does not provide important details such as the compartment for the black boxes which are visible on the real model — they have a canvas cover but this is usually pulled away as soon as the plane goes into action. So, we made a new piece for the black boxes, added new wiring and added a more detailed support for the canopy controller.

Once the cockpit was finished, we moved on to construct the compartments for which we had cut space right at the start (gun, nose cone and side compartments). We used 0.2mm plasticard glued with cyanoacrylate and added into the compartments anchorage points for the equipment we would be putting inside. Finally, we had to glue together the badly fitting fuselage pieces — these needed plenty of putty and sandpapering. Piece A-10, the back of the aircraft, is oversized and requires a lot of time (and sanding) to fit correctly. The wings, however, did not pose any problems.

After the general assembly phase, we worked on the radar equipment and the gun and ammunition feed, which we had

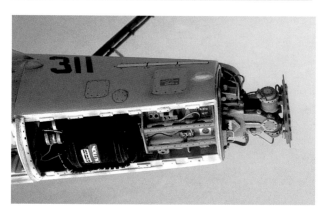

to build entirely from scratch, since the improvement kit only includes the antenna and the tracking mechanism; these elements were built — following photo references carefully — from materials such as squares and sections by Evergreen, plasticard and plastic rods of different thicknesses. The core of the ammunition feed is a plastic cylinder 5mm in diameter, the belt is built up from a base of aluminium sheet and 30 small pieces of plastic; wiring and transfers add the final touches. The colours are very similar to the real ones, with shading in the same darkened tone and highlights made with paler tones.

The undercarriage shafts did not escape our attention: the front one is incorrect — it is not deep enough, which is why we removed the original floor and all the wiring that the instructions showed. We made the dimensions of the compartment's walls and floor closer to reality and we added the necessary cables and structures; on the rear undercarriage we erased the entire original moulding and made a finer, more realistic one, following the photos. Next we painted the undercarriage white with 5% added black to give a slightly dirtied base colour, then we put on the transfers and finished by adding wear and tear with airbrushed black and brown inks (to dilute inks to shade, use a split of 8:2 alcohol to ink). The undercarriage struts posed no problems, as they were well detailed.

The wing transformation is complicated, and requires experience, good reference material and patience, too. The leading edge flaps were separated from the wing carefully with the internal face chamfered so that they could be lowered to about 30°. The trailing edge was more complex, because the manufacturer included part of the flap in the fuselage. This had to be cut out carefully and attached to the larger part of the flap we had already separated from the wing at the start. We rounded off the edge of the flap for attachment and removed with a 3mm file (approximately) the trailing edge of the wing.

After building eight small L-shaped pieces and fixing them onto the trailing edge, we covered them with a rectangular piece of plasticard 1mm thick, by 0.3mm wide, and the length of the wing.

The wing hinging was made from a 0.8mm plastic cylinder and plasticard; in total, 38 pieces were needed to complete each each wing.

PAINTING

The manufacturer's instructions show that the low visibility scheme has two tones, but in more up-to-date photography we can see that a single tone is the dominant scheme. We decided to airbrush with Tamiya acrylic paints, specifically Sky Grey (XF-22) plus 5% Light Blue; all varnished with Marabú gloss. The transfers (decals) are excellent and can be easily cut. there are a lot of them, too, although this is not the case with the current US Navy F-18s, which are extremely sparsely lettered. A coat of Marabú matt varnish gives the final finish.

For ageing, we used a mixed technique on the main body with airbrushed black ink and Post-it masks, and a 0.5mm brown sienna pencil. The hatches and small panels, grids and ventilation vents were painted in their original colours and slightly dirtied with sepia tones.

For the cowling we used the etched-brass from Verlinden

with the addition of cables and a new hydraulic controller. The nozzles were improved by adding the interior relief, painted steel grey (Humbrol no 54), darkened with graphite powder and shaded by airbrushing with black ink and sepia.

The weapons and avionics were from Verlinden, except for the containers of the laser detector and the infra-red scanner, which are the originals, but much improved with painting and transfer effects.

The weapon hardpoints were made of resin with etched-brass launching rails, plasticard clamps and scratch-built steel rods.

We left until last the refuelling probe and landing hook as they are very delicate pieces. The probe was scratch-built and the hook improved by making the original more precise and adding details

Our F-18C from USS *Constellation*'s VFA-192 'Golden Dragons' was based on our own photographic material supplemented by Verlinden's F-18 mongraph, as well as *Top Gun Fighters*, from Mallard Press.

The improved rear undercarriage units and compartments.

This model is made to a scale of ½, but is so well detailed it could easily pass for a larger scale such as ¼8.

Today it almost takes as long to model the weapons on a combat aircraft as it does to build the aircraft itself — all the missiles, containers, bombs, etc. As the F-18 can carry a bewildering array of multi- mission equipment, the variety of configurations is enormous. We finally opted for an anti-radar version, similar to that used during the Gulf War.

We left the central pylon empty (although we could have attached a cluster bomb) b detailed it by adding anchoring and pins. The wing pylons from the Verlinden kit are too thin have some inaccuracies, such as the poor relief and som blisters. The Hasegaw originals are a little rough, bu by smoothing them down wit sandpaper and adding detail such as the anchoring tiers an pins, they can be made to loo very realistic.

On the inside hardpoints w placed two auxiliary fuel tank which were painted in XF-19 with the exception of their nos cones, which were painted blac or pale yellow. For the oute hardpoints we had to scratch build the special HARM missi attachment, since neithe Hasewaga nor Verlinde provided one. We used a Evergreen section and based on photographic referenc material. The missile themselves posed no problem

Lid of the avionics hold and gun, cut out and built following the original.

The strut of the front undercarriage is profiled with pencil and slightly dirtied using an airbrush.

The compartment for the electronic equipment. This is composed of small sheets of acetate, copper wire and plastic sections from Evergreen.

The hydraulic pipes and articulations complete the undercarriage.

as their resin fuselage is magnificently made. We used fine bands of transfers (decals) on the etched-brass fins, following reference photos for the colour codes and drawing on details such as screws and rings in pencil. The insignia was dry transfers from Verlinden.

We filled the two empty stations on the fuselage with the laser and infra-red containers; these are used in bad weather and/or on night missions: they, too, posed no problems and fitted together perfectly. Lettering, transfers and fine paintwork details completed them.

The last task was to deal with the Sidewinders, since we had immediately thrown away the originals. An option was to use those from the 'Air-to-Air Armaments' box by Hasewaga, but when we compared the thickness of the fins (1mm at the roots) and took into account that the etched-brass fins of the HARM do not exceed 0.2mm, we felt we had no choice but to make new ones. We therefore used a rod from Evergreen, of the same thickness as the fuselage of a Hasewaga missile, and we rounded it off carefully to make the nose. For the fins we made up some Bristol board patterns which, once correctly sized, we used as a template on a 0.1mm plasticard sheet. Once they had all been drawn, we cut and glued

Detail on the wheels is emphasised with dry brush and airbrush inks.

The laser or infra-red container, as well as the tanks, occupy the inner hardpoints.

them carefully using a quick-drying paste and, (as with the HARMs) we used undecorated transfers for the bands and

details such as the fin rollers. They were painted grey (XF-19) with the nose darkened with the same colour plus 40% black.

The Sidewinder missile had to be made entirely from scratch.

The HARM missile comes from Verlinden and is made of resin with metal tabs.

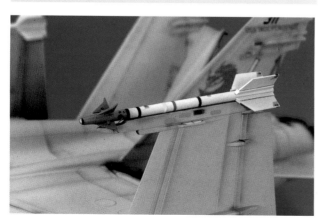

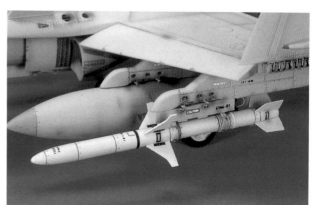

MiG-29 'FULCRUM'

Of all the Russian fighter planes, the MiG-29 is one of the most beautiful; with its soft lines and pure aerodynamic curves it produces a sensation of real harmony and dynamism. Since the opening up of the former USSR the documentation on the MiG has become enormous, allowing the super-detailing of this wonderful aircraft.

The Revell ⅓₅ scale model of the MiG-29 forms an excellent base from which to begin super-detailing work, because it only provides the exterior structure. As with the F-18 in the last section, the things we need to do are to super-detail the undercarriage and its compartments, the cockpit interior and avionics and weapons. The most useful reference for all this are books published by Verlinden — *Lock On*, no 19 — and Aerofax —

The completed assembly featuring the full reconstruction of the cockpit interior and the undercarriage legs.

The base coat is Pale Grey with Sky Grey (XF-19).

Both the upper and lower surfaces are painted the same grey.

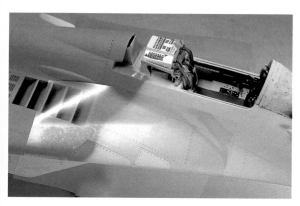

Adhesive masking was used to define the dark grey area.

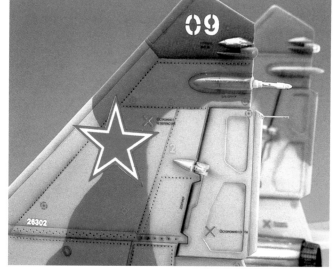

The tail shows the results of the laborious process of panelling and subtle dirtying.

View of the engine nozzles with their characteristic scorching.

Extra-2; these books show how everything is made using plasticard, strips, Evergreen squares, wire and metal sheets.

For the interior we have an excellent etched-brass kit from the Czechoslovak firm Eduard; nevertheless, it is still necessary to touch up the undercarriage, which involves complex and meticulous work on the wiring.

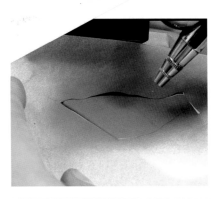

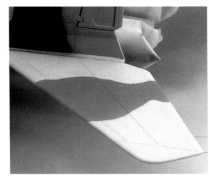

The green patches are made with the help of aircraft masks.

A mix of Flat White (XF-2), Medium Blue (XF-18) and Field Grey (XF-65) Tamiya acrylics were used.

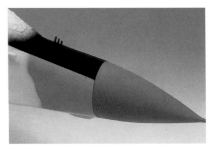

Anti-dazzle panel, masked with Letraline tape.

Nose cone painted with Tamiya Dark Grey (XF-24).

Elegant and simple green and grey camouflage.

PAINTING

Given the size and scale of this model, we had to carry out a particularly careful and extensive process of painting and weathering

General view, in which the harmonious and functional lines of the plane can be properly appreciated.

— as can be seen in photos, there are two versions of camouflage most commonly used. We have chosen the one with greens and greys, as we consider it the most attractive.

We began by covering the whole plane with Sky Grey (XF-19), using a spray gun containing well dissolved paint. By laying down the paint lightly in this way we avoided the granule effect — the sort of dusty granular look that sometimes appears — although we can, of course, rub down the paint with a cloth to pull off the granules while simultaneously polishing the surface.

The green camouflage patches are made with non-adhesive masks cut out of paper. First we sketched the outline of the piece to be painted, wings, rudder, etc; next we traced the patches following the schemes of the assembly plans, then cut out the parts to be painted. We stuck some pieces of cardboard under the edges of the paper so that the mask always remained proud of the scale model; in this way the edges of the markings will not be sharp, but slightly

First coat of colour — Chrome silver (X-11) from Tamiya.

Shades of blue, done with Holbein inks and dyes.

The first phase of painting is concluded, including the nozzles.

Second colour, with sepia, again from Holbein.

The last touches of colour, with black inks.

blurred. We used a mixture of Medium Blue (XF-18), Field Grey (XF-65) and Flat White (XF-2).

In front of the windscreen lies the anti-dazzle strip, which is painted matt black. We used flexible type tape Letraline to define the border and, at the same time, to retain the MiG-29's characteristic curvature. Care must be taken with the connection between the windscreen and the fuselage, because the transparent piece leaves a considerable hole, which must be filled with epoxy putty before painting.

The nozzles are an important feature and are

Overhead view to show the way that the panels and rivets have been emphasised overall with transparent sepia inks.

PANELLING AND WEATHERING

On such a large-scale model as this, the emphasising of panels and rivets, and weathering is fundamental (we only need to look at photographs to appreciate this). This stage was done in two steps: first we went over the aircraft panel by panel; we glued paper to the sides and used an airbrush to spray a sepia colour paint right in the middle of each panel, so the colour was very fine, only appearing on the unmasked area. This operation has to be done for the whole aircraft.

In the second phase, the airbrush is used with the hand raised, with the colour jet and the air flow at absolute minimum to obtain the finest possible line with which to emphasise the panels and rivets smoothly again. We then went on to make different markings on the underside of the aeroplane, the ailerons and, in general, on the areas that we can see as dirty in the photos of the actual aeroplane.

TRANSFERS (DECALS)

Once the panelling process is finished, the whole aeroplane is gloss varnished as a step prior to putting on the transfers. There are an awful lot of these

very rarely painted well. They are made of heat-resistant compound materials and develop distinctive 'oily' tones because of this heat. In the photographs, we can see metallic-looking colours made up of hazily attractive blues, browns and violets. To imitate

this appearance, we painted the whole piece silver; then, with an airbrush and transparent inks, applied blue and violet tones (the latter by mixing red and blue); then, finally, grey and brown to get the appropriate density. To finish, we applied a little metallic grey enamel with a dry brush.

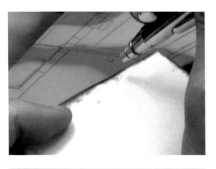

Rigid masks cut out of normal or Post-it type paper are used.

Some shading and weathering can be done with a raised hand.

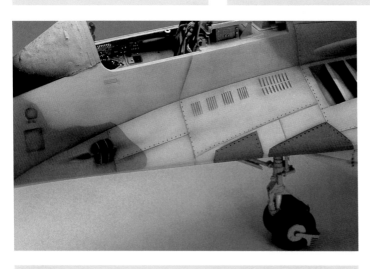

Once the emphasising of the panels is finished, the general weathering is done.

Plates, panels and special pieces, such as the chaff launchers, are weathered to look natural.

COLOUR CHART

GENERAL BASE
Sky Grey (Tamiya XF-19) acrylic

CAMOUFLAGE
Medium Blue (Tamiya XF-18)
Field Grey (Tamiya XF-65)
Flat White (Tamiya XF-2)

NOSE CONE AND SIDE PANELS
Dark Grey (Tamiya XF-24)

NOZZLES
Base: Chrome Silver (X11)
enamel. Blue, sepia, black.
Holbein transparent inks

PANELLING
Transparent sepia inks

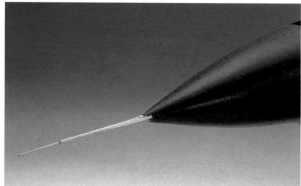

so great patience is needed to cut them out one by one, remove the transparent backing and, with the help of a brush, place them in the correct positions.

Once this laborious task is completed, the equipment is satin varnished — or even matt if appropriate.

The plane is gloss varnished completely before placing the transfers.

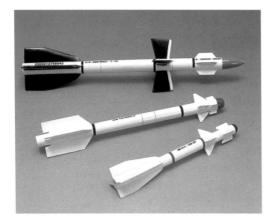

The missiles are painted white with bands of colour to identify the type to which they belong.

The underside has its general dirtiness more accentuated.

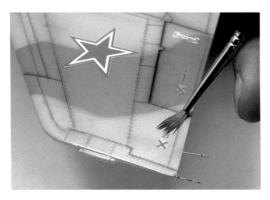

The placing of the transfers is a slow task, because they are so numerous.

Once all the lettering has been put on, apply a coat of satin varnish.

AV-8B HARRIER

In this article on the AV-8B Harrier we take you through step-by-step construction and super-detailing of the Monogram scale model (kit no 5448), using etched-brass accessories (no 7) from Todo Modelismo.

We began — as usual — by improving the cockpit. This is supplied by the maker with a baseboard on which the seat is included. This element is not very convincing, so we removed it using a knife and sandpaper. Later on we will reconstruct the bottom of this piece, including

The kit includes a single baseboard piece for the cockpit and the seat.

the rear structure and the ejection rails for the seat. Using plasticard we built the sides of the cockpit that form the seat hollow and placed etched-brass pieces 41 and 42 on the right and left respectively.

From the discarded seat we recovered the side pieces and headrests. Then, with plasticard, we built the floor and with strips

Using knife and sandpaper we removed the entire seat block.

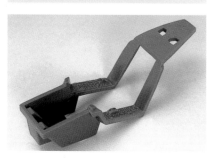

of acetate we improved the back, imitating the texture of the canvas with tin sheet, on which we engraved a soft relief with a fine knife.

The instrument panel in the kit contains dials and indicators already in place. However, it is unconvincing, so we removed the entire relief using a knife and file and used instead etched-brass piece no 4 from our sheet. We also eliminated the upper part of the board, since our etched-brass sheet includes pieces 21 and 21b, which form the edging of this piece. We finished the cockpit with the addition of piece 13 in the seat rear and the ejection handle (piece 18) in the lower front part of the seat.

With the model already

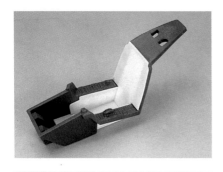

With 1mm plasticard we built the bottom and the floor.

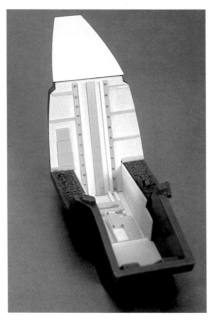

The seat piece is completed with additional detailing made from acetate and plasticard.

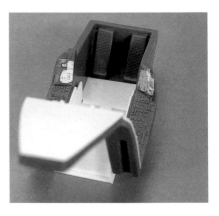

The two pieces (numbers 41 and 42), make up the instruments on the upper part of the consoles.

closed, we placed pieces 10 and 23 in the rear part; these form the tray with rail for the displacement of the cockpit canopy. The cockpit surround is completed with pieces 25 and 40, both belonging to the hood and its support.

Having reached this point, we went on to glue the wings

Piece 13 is part of the rear structure of the seat.

The ejection handle is situated at the rear; its number on the sheet is 18.

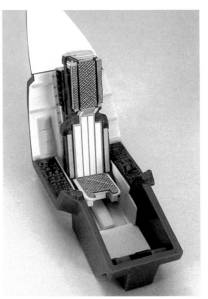

Once all the improvements to the the seat and base have been made it looks much more realistic.

We started by eliminating the original edging with a flat file.

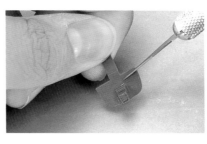

The remaining roughness is taken off using a sharp knife.

and stabilisers, filling the remaining holes with putty. Fitting the main bits together is the most complicated part of this model, and you will need a fair number of hours for the sanding process later as well.

The AV-8B has a system for increasing lift, consisting of a folding fin located behind the front undercarriage. The kit includes this element and its corresponding housing, but when we compared its shape with that of the real aircraft, we realised that it was wrong. We

First we fix the pieces (no 21 in the kit), that correspond to the instrument panel.

With piece 4 the instrument panel is ready to paint. The small frame, no 19, is the edge of the radar screen.

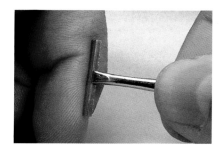

To bend piece no 23 we used flat mouth pincers.

Once piece 23 was bent, it was placed on no 10; the two form the back and slide rail of the cockpit canopy.

The cabin looks much better with all the elements added.

also need to prepare the fuselage to accommodate the etched-brass pieces. We made a paper template for the fin, copied it on plasticard and, using a knife, cut the correct shapes. Pieces 44, 43, 22 and 2 made up the structure of the fin.

The front undercarriage shaft and the airbrake housing also need to be completed with plasticard, and bottoms added, to serve as support for etched-

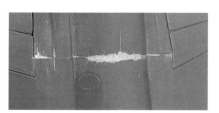

The scale model needs good work with putty and sandpaper in some areas, as there are problems fitting the pieces together neatly.

Under piece 10 we fitted a plasticard sheet and various elements to give volume to the area.

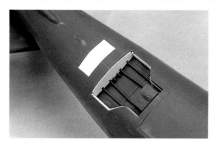

The area of the airbrake and the flare dispenser have been improved with pieces of plasticard.

Small details made with very fine plasticard complete the nozzles and the front undercarriage.

The fit of the auxiliary undercarriage is levelled with a small piece cut to the correct shape.

Piece 20 is the flare launcher; on its two sides are two low-intensity lighting strips (no 8).

brass piece no 20, — the chaff dispenser.

Etched-brass pieces nos 8 and 9 correspond to the low intensity lights for flying in formation. Our sheet supplies eight of these — the small ones are distributed along the fuselage and the two larger ones located on the tail. We removed the lights that are engraved on

the fuselage, using first the tip of a knife, then finished the surface with a very fine file. The etched-brass pieces were fixed later using slow drying cyanoacrylate. For pieces 29 and 20b (the reaction nozzles located in the tail), we carried out the same procedure as for the low intensity lights. The fuselage is completed with pieces 30 (the

two small fences located on the leading edges of the wings), 36, (the frame of the air intake for the APU system and the blade antenna), then, finally, pieces 7 and 14, which complete the placing of all the fuselage etched-brass super-detailing.

The Todo Modelismo sheet contains 15 elements for detailing the undercarriage.

Using a sharp knife we removed part of the lighting strip detail.

Using a very fine file (minimum 600) we filed down the area completely.

The etched-brass piece is fitted using slow drying cyanoacrylate.

The pieces numbered no 34 form the undercarriage auxiliary legs. To fit them, we removed the plastic originals, making instead a support of small plasticard bars. No 35 pieces replace the rings engraved on the legs of the undercarriage; the sheet includes six units, although we only used four. We also used piece no 17 as a ring on the taxying light, found on the leg of the front undercarriage.

The most delicate operation when putting on the etched-brass pieces is undoubtedly with the perspex pieces. We began with the cockpit canopy, removing with a 600 or 800 file all traces of rims and explosive cable. After this operation the cockpit canopy is opaque, but it quickly regains all its former transparency after a gentle polish with Tamiya compound and cotton. But before doing this glue the frames, pieces nos 31, 27, 37 and 33, as well as the rear-view mirrors, and the cable, (piece no 12) into place.

The hollow for the folding aerodynamic element is supplied with an incorrect shape, so needs to be rectified.

By superimposing a thin sheet of paper we obtained a transfer with the approximate dimensions.

The transfer was then used as a template to cut a piece of plasticard to fit the hollow.

Using a thin tipped knife we hollowed out the piece, giving the interior the right shape.

After fitting the piece in the fuselage, we fitted point 1 inside it with small rail no. 3.

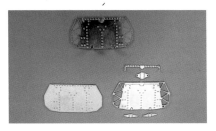

At the top is the complete aerodynamic element, with its corresponding piece below, (pieces 42, 44, 22 and 2).

On the upper part of the fuselage are the two lighting strips (no. 8) and the APU outlet (piece 26).

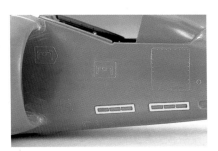

Pieces no. 8 on the sides of the cockpit and blade antenna (no. 16) on the lower part.

Piece no. 29, shaped with the process described above, fits almost perfectly.

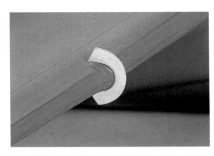

The two 'fence' pieces are fixed using slow drying cyanoacrilate (piece no. 30).

The flashing weathercock fixed on the nose (piece no. 6).

Blade antenna on the back of the plane. (piece no. 1)

To curve the fins of the ventilation grid (piece no 36) we use flat-mouthed pincers.

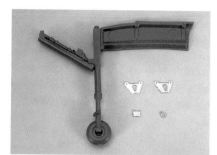

The now bare auxiliary undercarriage is prepared to be completed with pieces no. 34 for the articulations, and no. 35 for the rings for securing in the cowling.

Complete undercarriage. Apart from the etched-brass pieces, some areas have been improved with bits of plasticard.

For the leg of the front undercarriage we have a circular ring (piece 17) that is part of the taxying light, which also has two securing rings (no 35).

The cockpit canopy has the frames and explosive cable engraved; to remove them we filed them down with at least an 800 grain file.

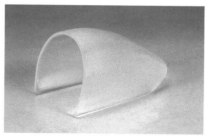

After filing down the cockpit canopy, it has a totally opaque finish.

After cleaning the cockpit canopy, its appearance is perfect.

On the lower part of the cockpit canopy we placed pieces no. 37.

After fitting the arches (pieces 27 and 31), we proceeded to put on the explosive cable (piece 12), using slow drying cyanoacrylate in very small quantities to glue it.

The interior arch (piece 33) serves in turn as support for the rear-view mirrors (piece no 5).

Etched-brass pieces 24 and 28 are for the arches of the windscreen; for the side windows we used numbers 39.

The windscreens use pieces 24, 39 and 38, including four of the latter; only a pair of these is used, so we can choose between the two types. We used slow drying cyanoacrylate in very small quantities, to avoid dulling the plastic something easily caused by the drying adhesive vapours.

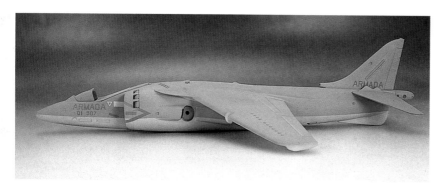

With the two general colours applied as well as the lettering, the model is ready for the weathering process.

The undercarriage recesses and the hollow for the airbrake have been painted in matt white.

Once the etched-brass pieces have been fitted, we prepared the model for painting, masking and protecting the relevant areas. We started by airbrushing Grey H-308 from Gunze Sangyo (FS-36375) on the upper parts, and on the lower areas a mix of 95% Matt White (H-11) and 5% Matt Black (H-12). The lettering and numbering was done using masks cut earlier, and coloured using 85% Grey (H-308), darkened with 15% matt black.

The emblems of the Navy and the Spanish cockades are transfers by Hobby Calcas (ref 21).

To age the paintwork, we shaded the panels with an airbrush, using the edge of plain paper or adhesive as a mask, — depending on the area concerned — and well diluted matt black. For the low intensity lighting strips, the sidelights, etc, the detailed painting is done with a brush.

The undercarriage is one of the most detailed parts of the Monogram kit, and includes wiring and cabling. To paint it we used matt white.

Finally we assembled the most delicate and fiddly elements, such as the airbrakes

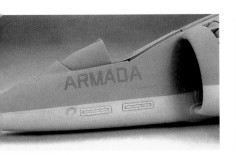

The Navy lettering is painted on at an early stage using an adhesive mask; the numbers were painted later using the same system.

The painting is completed by adding the boxes and stencils; both have been done using airbrush and masking.

The Navy insignia has been put on using a transfer (decal), prior to the varnishing process.

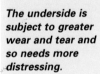

The low visibility lights have been decorated with acrylic lemon yellow from Marabú.

After the weathering process, the model is ready to be varnished.

The underside is subject to greater wear and tear and so needs more distressing.

struts we used Khaki Yellow (Vallejo 976) with a mild wash of Black (950).

As a final detail, we added the sidelights and painted them with translucent Tamiya acrylics. Also the fairings for the radar alert system, these are situated on the margin rims and are coloured pale yellow.

One of the best parts of the kit is the undercarriage since it includes almost all the elements as standard.

The front undercarriage and the auxiliary units are also completed with pieces of etched-brass.

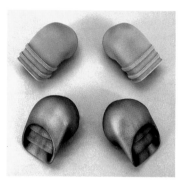

The nozzles have been decorated using Holbein transparent inks in sepia, black, orange and blue on a matt aluminium base.

The model is finished with cables for the electrical system and many stencils.

and the aerodynamic deflector which is located behind the front undercarriage. The scale model was completed with the installation of the weaponry and the external tanks — which happily posed no problems in their assembly or painting.

We had to take special care when gluing the cockpit canopy — it has to be fixed with a slow drying adhesive. To paint the

Subtle weathering on the wings; real aircraft are subject to considerable wear and tear.

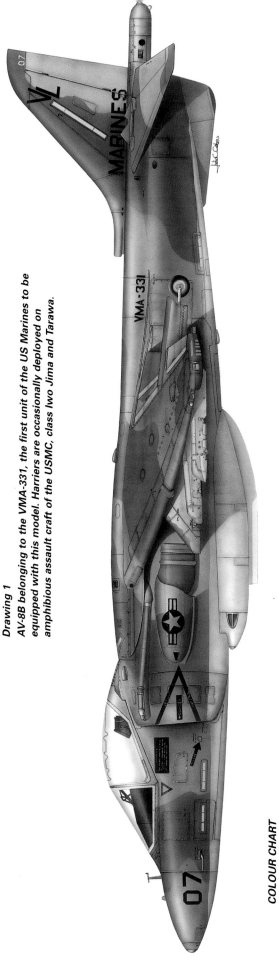

Drawing 1

AV-8B belonging to the VMA-331, the first unit of the US Marines to be equipped with this model. Harriers are occasionally deployed on amphibious assault craft of the USMC, class Iwo Jima and Tarawa.

COLOUR CHART

Upper areas: *Grey (Gunze Sangyo H-308)*

Lower areas: *95% Matt White (Tamiya XF-2)and 5% Matt Black (Tamiya XF-1)*

Panelling: *Very dilute Matt Black (XF-1)*

Cockpit canopy struts: *Khaki yellow (Vallejo 976)*

Low intensity lights: *Yellow (Marabú 020)*

Finish: *Marabú satin varnish*

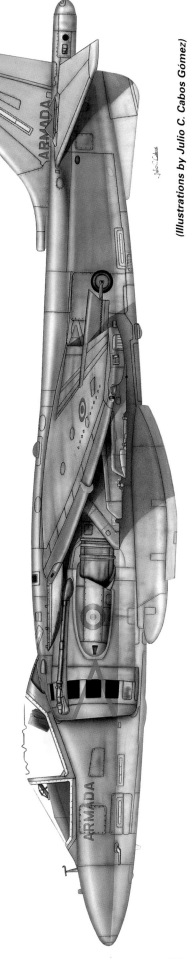

Drawing 2

AV-8B belonging to the Spanish Navy. The planes of the 9th Squadron sport a low visibility colour scheme, based on grey tones.

(Illustrations by Julio C. Cabos Gómez)

The small elements, such as the pitot tube, are put on at the very end of the process.

The rear radome contains two small radar alert antennas and a small luminous beacon that is not included in the kit.

The weathering of the underside of the fuselage must be done with special care to show damage from the heat of the nozzles.

The in-flight refuelling point is fixed on the left side, adding an appearance of technical complexity to this area of the plane.

The red elements on the weaponry are part of the security system.

The grids on the upper fuselage have been painted matt black with a soft dry brush then dusted with grey.

The aerodynamic deflector contains the '07' corresponding to the last two digits of the aircraft number. In this case they have been painted by hand.

The weaponry on the scale model is correct, only the fins on the Sidewinders needed additional work (see article on F-18C).

TORNADO F Mk 3

The Hasegawa kit comes complete with many details, but there is still scope to improve a satisfying number of aspects — such as improving the detailing on both sides of the fuselage, the undercarriage shaft and the missile fairings. However, all in all, the kit is a first class base for carrying out super-detailing work.

For this job we need plenty of good references and lots of patience. We worked on the cockpit, gun compartment, refuelling probe, radar cone, air intakes, slats, flaps, spoilers, airbrakes and undercarriage shafts.

Using a fine saw we began by cutting away the radar cone, the gun compartment and the refuelling probe, as well as the auxiliary air intakes. Moving on to the cockpit, we built the side structures of the cockpit with 0.1mm plasticard, painting these with a medium grey, so that later — with a paler tone — we could create detail with a dry brush. Then we added the wiring and lettering. We moved on to make

the instrument panels with different thickness plasticard and, again, created detail and shape with a dry brush. The instrumentation details were painted using muted red and yellow tones. We then improved the seats by adding buckles, belts, cabling and rails for the ejection seat. When the cockpit

The radar cone is cut with a fine saw.

was finished, we moved on to the undercarriage bays, which we detailed by adding pieces painted in white matt toned down with grey and washed with a mixture of brown and black oil

Front bay, to which detailing has been added.

After opening the gun compartment, the different components must be made with very fine plastic sheet and metal wire.

To ensure that the backing for the transfers (decals) is not noticeable, we gloss-varnished the entire plane.

at a ratio of 80-20%; later we added the hydraulic circuits, made with 0.2mm and 0.3mm copper wire and painted different shades of green and black.

Next we worked on the gun and the refuelling probe; carefully following the photos, we built both using plasticard, copper and steel wire. Small lettering and wiring added realism.

We detailed the seats inside the cockpit by adding the ejection seat rails, belts and buckles as well as the complex system of cables.

The biggest problem with ½ scale is reducing the size of the pieces, which become too big as soon as they are altered.

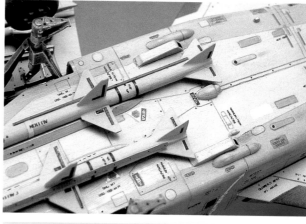

The finer details are usually omitted from mass-produced scale models, so it is necessary to add hydraulic levers, support hooks and most of the ribs.

Once this phase is finished, we added the bulkhead (which we used as a support for the radar equipment) and moved on to the most complicated job — the transformation of the wings, an operation we performed very carefully following all available photos and plans. We cut away the original flaps and prepared the spoilers using a very fine saw and sandpaper.

We also prepared the leading edge to house the slat and its corresponding rails. The Fowler type flaps need their respective guides, unfolding mechanisms and intermediate sheets. Lastly, we detailed the internal structures of the airbrakes, their cables and circuits, and added the hatches of the auxiliary air intakes and their hydraulic actuators.

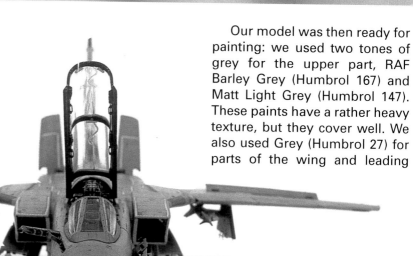

Our model was then ready for painting: we used two tones of grey for the upper part, RAF Barley Grey (Humbrol 167) and Matt Light Grey (Humbrol 147). These paints have a rather heavy texture, but they cover well. We also used Grey (Humbrol 27) for parts of the wing and leading

The cockpit closing handles are made with very fine metal sheets or metal wire.

The fins of the missiles are replaced with other thinner ones.

The feeling of complexity — so much a part of modern aircraft — is almost tangible; the large amount of lettering contributes to this.

The panelling is emphasised with brown 0.5mm sheet.

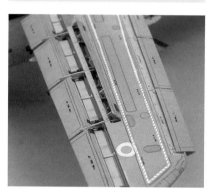

The flaps had to be cut to get the correct trim for the wings.

edge fairing. Once dry, we proceeded to paint some access panels in their base colour, but darkened with 10% black, in an alternating and asymmetric way.

We panelled the scale model with pencil, using a brown refill (Marsmicrocrohm sienna 0.5mm) and a flexible template in the more complicated areas; in this way, the model gets a used and realistic look. We finished the painting with details such as navigation

lights (Tamiya translucent colour), the antenna fairings and small radomes (matt black and hemp yellow), and metallic areas (Humbrol Metal Cote).

The transfer (decal) sheet is well made and offers a choice between three different versions of the Tornado F3, with all the material a modeller could need. We decided to use the most striking set of transfers (decals)

— those belonging to No 65 Squadron, part of 11 Group, RAF.

We cut away the transparent parts of transfers, cutting around the squadron crest, tactical markings and insignia with a very sharp knife; once dry the transfers are varnished individually with Humbrol Satin Cote. The lettering on the sheet is replaced with one

All the numbers and insignia had to be cut out carefully so as to leave as little of the transparent backing as possible. Once all the transfers were correctly in place, the entire aircraft was varnished with Humbrol Satin Cote.

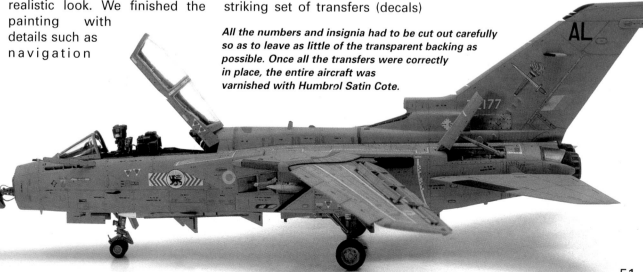

from Verlinden that uses dry transfers.

When the painting phase was finished, we attached the heavily detailed undercarriage units. The flaps were made from 3mm plasticard then smoothed and shaped with fine files and Tamiya sandpaper.

The radar system has to be fitted right at the end, as it is an extremely delicate element; the weaponry, composed of four BAe Skyflashes and two Sidewinders — on which the original fins are replaced with ones made from plasticard — give the finishing touch to the model.

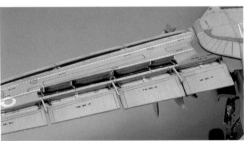

The metallic areas are painted with Humbrol Metal Cote, mixed with brown.

All the grooves and channelling on the wings are reconstructed with fine sheets and metal wire.

We chose a simple painting scheme so as not to detract from the large amount of lettering and the extremely complex super-detailing.

Bibliography:
Tornado, Francis K. Mason
Warbirds Illustrated
   No. 42, Michael J. Gething.

PANAVIA TORNADO — GRAPHIC REPORT

The Tornado, the result of collaboration between old enemies such as the Germany, the United Kingdom and Italy, is undoubtedly one of the most potent arms systems in NATO; its original programme dates back to 1967.

Initially the international collaboration for the Tornado was limited to West Germany and Canada as main manufacturers, with Belgium, Italy and the Netherlands also added as a consequence of the need to reduce costs in their own defence programmes. Then, and because of the British-French failure to produce a combined fighter, the United Kingdom group was also added. They needed to find a change for their considerably outdated English Electric Canberras. Finally, the desertion of the Canadians, followed by that of the Belgians and Dutch, ended up leaving the UK, Germany and Italy as the only partners.

The Panavia Tornado is a multi-purpose aeroplane in its widest possible meaning. The performance characteristics forced the adoption of variable geometry (from 25° in a forward position up to 68° with the maximum deflection), in order to endow it with the designated flight and landing speeds.

To reach the speeds required,

Rear view of the starboard undercarriage and its external doors.

Detail of the starboard 27mm Mauser gun and the Laser Ranger Marked Target Seeker.

it was necessary to design new engines and, as a consequence, the RB-199-34B, 7,255kg static drive turbofan made its appearance in the aeronautical world.

The official performance characteristics of this aeroplane are calculated as: maximum speeds at sea level: 1,482km/h (Mach 1.25) and 2,600km/h (Mach 2.2), at its maximum ceiling of 21,000m.

Its weights are 13,600kg

Interesting view of the starboard undercarriage nacelle, (left) showing the opening and closing devices and the folding/opening device for the undercarriage. At right the operation of the trailing edge flaps is clarified.

empty and 27,210kg maximum at take-off. The span depends on the angle of incidence of the variable geometry wings: 8.60m at maximum deflection and 13.9m at minimum deflection.

The offensive carrying capability is about 9,000kg, depending on the mission, and on the type of weaponry for that particular mission. As fixed they mount two 27mm guns (ground attack) or one on the air defence version. On the underwing pylons (also with variable geometry) Tornado can carry anything from anti-ship

missiles, such as the Kormoran or Sea Eagle, and air to surface weapons such as the AS 30/30L to all types of electronic warfare pods, iron bombs, laser-guided bombs etc. The aircraft that participated in the war against Iraq were equipped with ALE40/ON flare and chaff dispensers.

The aircraft shown here is a Panavia Tornado GR1/1DA Co-Interdiction-Strike) for land/sea attacks, against nerve centres and as frighteners (the epithet most often used in the war against Iraq was 'anti-strike', a typical US martial expression), from the British No 27 Squadron, with its usual two-colour camouflage — irregular strips of Dark Sea Grey and Dark Green. These photos were taken

in May 1992 at the Airex-92 show in half an hour. At other times and places the livery and markings would be different.

Detail of the rudder.

SUKHOI Su-27 'FLANKER B'

The Sukhoi Su-27 is an aircraft with elegant and aggressive lines, making it a model that all modern jet enthusiasts must have in their collection.

This Su-27 comes from Hasegawa (kit ref. K-40) and is of very good quality. It includes a number of white metal parts such as the landing gear, seat, various actuators, etc; and a small amount of etched-brass—such as grilles for the ventilation grids.

The least satisfactory aspect of the model are the transfers (decals). Although there are a lot of them and they are accurate, they provide for only a single version of the aircraft — so there is no choice (but perhaps we are spoilt after the excellent

Tornado). The kit comes without accessories for additional detailing, but luckily can be improved with some of the accessories available on the market, such as the Eduard etched-brass set, True Details KM-38 seat and Hi-Decals

The original missiles in the kit were replaced by those supplied in a Dragon kit. They were painted gloss white, with various black and silver details.

The rear area of the fuselage must have a metallic finish, using subtly varied tones to differentiate the panels.

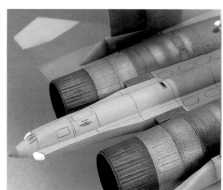

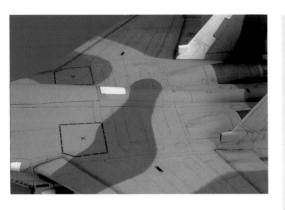

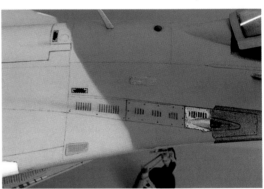

We used Bristol board templates for the painting, slightly raising the edges of the board to achieve a slightly blurred edge.

The white areas on the fins were defined by using adhesive masks.

A hint of wear and tear emphasises the ventilation grids.

transfers. The Verlinden monograph from the 'Lock On' series provided the references for super-detailing the model.

We started with the assembly of the cockpit, painting its interior with pale grey (Humbrol M-147), the side consoles with black and the buttons and controls with grey and white. The seat is entirely black.

Inside the etched-brass head-up display we inserted a small piece of transparent acetate to imitate glass. The cockpit canopy mechanism was painted dark earth (Humbrol M-29).

The glass is correctly

THE Su-27 FLANKER MODELS *(injection-moulded plastic kits currently being produced)*		
Brand	**Reference**	**Scale**
ACADEMY	2131	1/48
AIRFIX	5025	1/72
HASEGAWA	K-40	1/72
HELLER	80371	1/72
HELLER	80550	1/72
ITALERI	187	1/72
ITALERI	197	1/72
DRAGON	4576	1/144
ITALERI	881	1/144
REVELL	04084	1/144

moulded, but there is a seam where the moulds joined. To

eliminate this, we first rubbed with fine grade 600 sandpaper, then polished the canopy with Tamiya Compound and the help of a mini-drill, covering the end of the bit with cotton. This is a delicate task, since the rubbing causes the plastic to heat up, and it may deform or melt if polished carelessly or hurriedly. You must clean slowly.

The area that can be most improved by detailing is the undercarriage legs and wheel bays. Using thin plastic we added various pieces, and we simulated electrical wiring and hydraulics with copper wire. The

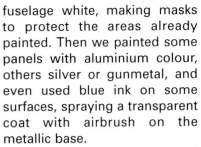

The interior of the air intakes and the nozzles is painted in a characteristic pale cream tone.

fuselage white, making masks to protect the areas already painted. Then we painted some panels with aluminium colour, others silver or gunmetal, and even used blue ink on some surfaces, spraying a transparent coat with airbrush on the metallic base.

The painting was completed once the radome and various antennas were finished. The

The undercarriage has been improved with small details, such as the copper wire hydraulic systems. Note the red colour inside the hatches.

wheel bays were painted with the same pale grey as inside the cockpit, although the hatches are a bright red colour. The insides of the air intakes were painted matt cream (M-103).

The camouflage is made up of the three colours that the Xtracolor provides for this aircraft: X-601, X-602 and X-603. This paint is applied using Bristol board templates — but remember to raise the edges of the boards to blur the edges of the colours. After applying the camouflage, there is still a lot of work necessary to complete the paint job: we painted the metallic areas on the rear of the

wheel hubs were painted in X-628 from Xtracolor.

Before putting on the transfers, we emphasised the lines of the panels with a pencil and the joints of the ailerons with sepia ink and airbrush. The model was then given a matt varnish, except for the metallic areas, which needed a satin finish.

Next we added the weapons, using missiles supplied in the Dragon kit Modern Soviet Weapons No 1, since they are better quality than those included with the original model, particularly the R-73 missiles. All these were painted gloss white with some details silver and black.

COLOUR CHART

Cockpit and undercarriage interiors: Pale Grey (Humbrol M-147)
Interior of nozzles: Matt Cream (Humbrol M-103)
Camouflage: X-601, X-602, X-603 all from Xtracolor
Radome: Matt White (Humbrol 34)
Missiles: Gloss White (Humbrol 22)

One of the most delicate operations is removing the small rough edge at the join of the two moulds used to make the cockpit canopy.

An ordinary well sharpened pencil is ideal for emphasising the lines of the panels.

The joints of the ailerons were emphasised using an airbrush and sepia ink.

SUKHOI Su-24 'FENCER'

Traditionally considered the Soviet version of the F-111, the Su-24 'Fencer' is a very capable supersonic bomber, capable of performing a wide variety of missions.

The Su-24 project began in 1965, at a time when the Soviet air forces needed to replace the outdated Il-28 and Yak-28B. Accordingly, they issued a series of requirements for a new multi-purpose attack aircraft. In response, the Sukhoi technical office designed a two-seat twin-engined machine, with side-by-side seating and a fixed wing configuration; it was also fitted with a number of small vertical lift engines for deployment in a very small space. This prototype was named the T-6, and flew for the first time on 2 July 1967. After intensive testing, the vertical lift engines were rejected, with a new variable-geometry wing being installed in their place: a more reliable and feasible concept.

Mass-production began in Novosibirsk in late 1971, and the Su-24 entered service in 1973. Fitted with state-of-the-art navigation and attack systems, the 'Fencer' caused a sensation within NATO, whose analysts reported that it could run rings round Western defenses, thanks

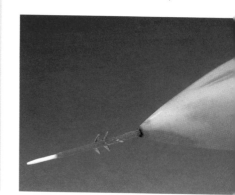

Left air intake on the Su-24MR. Visible under it is the reconnaissance chamber.

The reworked pitot tube, with front end etched-brass detailing of its small sensors.

to its terrain-following radar system and its panoply of new laser-guided weapons. From 1980 the Su-24s began to be deployed in various bases in East Germany, so its range of action covered the whole of Europe.

Between 1975 and 1976, as the result of experience gained through operational use and research done by Sukhoi's own design team, trials were made with updated avionics equipment and navigation systems.

Designated Su-24M, the new aircraft became the first with an in-flight refuelling probe, allowing 'buddy' refuelling from the small ventral tank of another Su-24. The most obvious external change was the nose which was lengthened to 750mm.

The first flight of the Su-24M took place during July 1977. This model served as the basis for the Su-24MK, a less sophisticated version for the export market, sold to the air

forces of Libya, Syria, Iraq and Iran.

The Su-24MR reconnaissance version (or 'Fencer E') does not

Note the difference in colour between the pure white and off-white of the front cone.

Cockpit detail. (Photo: Karl-Heinz Feller)

The cockpit interior is much improved with the resin seats and various etched-brass details.

have the 30mm cannon, but in its place it has oblique and panoramic cameras as well as lateral radars, infra-red sensors and a TV camera. It differs externally from the Su-24M on account of the small hump on the dorsal view.

The last version identified is for electronic reconnaissance, and named the 'Fencer F'. This aircraft does not have attack radar, incorporating in its place a large quantity of passive electronic systems to classify and disrupt enemy radar.

The first combat the Sukhoi Su-24 saw occurred during the Soviet occupation of Afghanistan. Around April 1984, these planes precision-bombed rebel positions at altitudes of over 5,000m, but without any opposition. During the Gulf War, all the Iraqi Su-24s took refuge on Iranian territory. Around this

The lower surfaces of the fuselage have been improved with various etched-brass accessories. The wheels are by Avia Equipage. As can be seen, the model needs the application of putty and then the sandpapering of almost all connection points.

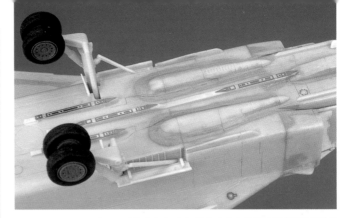

This is the finish of one of the two Kh-31 missiles.

The interior of a recon Fencer. There are a surprisingly large number of analog instruments in the cockpit.

This view allows an appreciation of the details of the moving parts of the cockpit canopy.

time the Iranian Air Force began to use the Su-24, acquiring more 'Fencers' from the Ukraine.

The most recent conflict in which the Su-24 has intervened is the war in Chechnya. During the winter of 1994, they were used to destroy all the bridges around the capital Grozny. Another spectacular action was the bombing of the leader of the independence movement, who was located when he used his mobile phone. The subsequent bombing with KAB-1500 laser bombs caused his death.

THE SCALE MODEL

The scale model illustrated is a Sukhoi Su-24M 'Fencer D' from the current Dragon catalogue (ref. 2502); there is also an Italeri 'Fencer C' available, a slightly different aircraft with a shorter nose.

The general quality of the kit is good; however, a comparison against reliable plans confirms that, although the lines of the existing panels are well reproduced, there are many

Reinforcements and details are made with small plastic strips and sheets.

Small details added to the rear were all made with plastic.

others missing. The interior of the cockpit is rather sparse, a problem that can be solved with the etched-brass details from Eduard. The original seats were replaced by True Details resin ones. The wheels were also changed, using resin hubs and black rubber tyres made by the Russian company Avia Equipage.

ASSEMBLY

As is usual with many scale aircraft, we started by making the cockpit. The base colour for

Detail of the front undercarriage (Photo: Karl-Heinz Feller).

the whole interior and also for the instrument panel is pale bluish grey (Humbrol M-175).

To the movable part of the cockpit canopy we had to add numerous details, made of plastic of different thicknesses, to simulate various metal pieces and plates. When mounting some of the other elements such as the radar screen and the pilot's viewfinder, extra care must be taken so that they do not scrape against the front of the cockpit. The instruments, some panels and the seats were Matt Black (M-33) in colour. In the specific case of the seats, the harnesses were painted pale grey (M-28) and other details yellow, white and red.

On the fuselage and near the tail-fin are the chaff/flare-launchers. These had been omitted from the kit and we got them from the Italeri Ka-50 helicopter model.

When mounting the main elements — such as the fuselage and tailplanes — we need to counterbalance the nose and check that the position of the wings can be adjusted without any problems.

The wings of this Dragon Su-24 kit can be multi-positioned, although some model makers prefer to glue them in a specific

pose. Next we started the thankless task of engraving the missing panel lines and details; this can be done with a scriber or with a thick needle, together with the engraving templates produced by Verlinden in etched brass. The engraved details are touched up later with a fine brush, dampened in solvent to soften the resulting effect. Finally, we sanded all the surfaces with a very fine grained paper.

On the exterior of the aircraft we needed to add antennas, air intakes and sensors. The in-flight refuelling probe is moulded to be mounted in deployed position, which is not very attractive. To place it in its usual position, we cut it in half and inserted it in its housing.

Pieces C54 and C55 create an edge when fitted, so putty has to be applied to the whole outline and then sanded back.

The front undercarriage has a very narrow mudguard which hinders the fitting of the new wheels, so their width had to be increased by about 1.5mm. The interior of the shafts and gates, as well as the axles of the undercarriage, were painted grey (S-129). The weapons included with the model were varied, but therewas only one of each, which is not very realistic or practical. In this case we opted to place a pair of large

The white and grey outlines where the colours meet must be blurred a little to look authentic.

Italeri Kh-31 anti-radar missiles, from the Su-24 kit. When mounting these missiles, we had to make their central pod as it is not supplied on any of the scale models. Its construction is straightforward enough, except that it requires fiddly work with sheets of plastic and putty and then lots of sanding back.

PAINTING

Matt White (M-34) was applied after masking the transfers to the underside surfaces and the nose. Then, after protecting the areas already painted, Pale Grey (Humbrol S-127) — the closest tone to the real Su-24 — was applied to the remainder. The borders between the grey and white do not have hard edges but — as is usual practice — they are slightly blurred; this effect is achieved by careful airbrushing with templates positioned a short distance from the surface. The white of the radome and the antennas are imitated with medium white, to which a drop of cream (Humbrol M-103) is added. The contrast must be very soft.

The interior of the engine nozzles is also painted black, mixed, in this case, with a touch of red. After a first coat of gloss varnish we emphasised the lines of panels and details with pencil. The pencil is graphite on the grey parts and ochre on the white — so as not to over-emphasise. After adding the transfers, the entire plane is varnished with a matt finish.

When the Fencer has missiles or fuel tanks of large dimensions mounted on it, the plane has large pylons. (Photo: Karl-Heinz Feller).

The 'Zfir' reconnaissance pod mounted on the Su-24MR. (Photo: Karl-Heinz Feller).

The Kh-31 missiles are painted with a combination of orange, red and various metallic tones, which is how they were painted before entering mass-production and while they were still on test.

These missiles and their corresponding pylons, as well as small antennas, probes, etc, are mounted at the last possible moment because they are so fragile.

One of the major difficulties of this model is the work of engraving all the omitted structural details. In the subsequent painting process, they are highlighted with pencil.

The black colour inside the nozzles has been mixed with some red.